I'M AN ADDICT
IN BITS AND PIECES

ONE WOMAN'S JOURNEY

By Shamin Brown

Goldrock Press
Norway House, Manitoba, Canada

Copyright © 2014 by Shamin Brown

Published by Goldrock Press
www.goldrockpress.com

Printed and bound in Canada by ArtBookbindery
www.artbookbindery.com

Cover Design by Yvonne Parks
Copy Edit by Audrey Dorsch

This book may not be reproduced, scanned, or distributed in any printed or electronic form without permission from the publisher, except in the case of brief quotations embodied in critical articles or reviews.

This book is a true account as written by the author based on her memories of events. Goldrock Press will not be held responsible for any liability resulting from the publication of these accounts. Some names have been changed to respect the privacy of family members and friends.

Scripture quotes are taken from THE HOLY BIBLE, NEW INTERNATIONAL VERSION®, NIV® Copyright © 1973, 1978, 1984, 2011 by Biblica, Inc.® Used by permission. All rights reserved worldwide.

Library and Archives Canada Cataloguing in Publication

Brown, Shamin, 1979-, author
    I'm an addict : in bits-- and pieces / Shamin Brown.

ISBN 978-1-927410-17-2 (pbk.)

    1. Brown, Shamin, 1979-. 2. Drug addicts--Canada--Biography. 3. Drug addicts--Religious life--Canada. 4. Drug abuse--Religious aspects--Christianity. I. Title.

HV5805.B765A3 2014   362.29'3092   C2014-900027-8

DEDICATION

This book is written in honor of the Lord who loved me enough to stop me from being what I wasn't and opened my eyes to who I am.

It is dedicated to the addict who still suffers and the little girl inside the women who have yet to find themselves... don't give up until the miracle happens. We believe in you!

This book is also dedicated to Dustin and my three sons. I am grateful for your love and your lives each waking moment.

THANK YOU

To Aretha Johnson, Carrie Winslow, Lise Campagne, Tammy Walker, and my mom, Maria Sherman for believing in me until I found the courage to believe in myself and for your constant love and exhortation.

To Dave Montgomery and John Kendrick of Kendrick Quality Printing for your generous contributions to the early stages of this project. Thank you for your kind words, your trust, and your ever ready encouragement.

A special thank you to my Aunt Lily for all her help in typing the manuscript.

Thank you for believing I could make a difference. Many blessings to you all!

NOTE TO THE READER

This book is based on journal entries written over the first five years of Shamin's recovery. It is the publisher's hope that these entries will be helpful to those currently struggling with addictions, and to those who would seek to help them.

Because there are graphic details included in this book, memories may surface for those who have been abused as children. It is important for you to realize that you are not alone! It was not your fault – you were a child. As a child, you did not have the ability to process being hurt by those you loved and trusted. As an adult, you do have the ability to process this hurt but you need to do it slowly and with the help of trained counsellors.

To know Jesus is to know the Great Healer. He only asks us to trust Him – a simple but often difficult decision for those who have been betrayed by someone they should have been able to trust. Life here on earth may be difficult, but it is a journey we all must take. There is Someone who wants to walk beside us. Someone whose love for us is perfect. As you open yourself up to Him, He will speak truth to your mind and to your heart – and He will set you free.

GROUP USE GUIDE

The discussion questions in this book are intended for self-reflection by the reader. If used in a group setting, the chapter can be read followed by guided group-led discussion. Everyone present – group members, staff, family and facilitator – should fully participate. I called this shared healing. I believe shared healing makes the space sacred and is central to building shame resilience. It is crucial that the facilitator has life experience that they can draw from to connect with the group. It is also essential that all group members have access to a professional counsellor to follow up with outside of the group.

As a facilitator, it is important to be flexible and adapt to the group. Never push for responses without adapting the questions to fit the group's comfort level. As examples, you might ask for one word that they would use to describe the chapter, or what they felt as they listened, or any thoughts or memories that arose during the reading. If the group is quiet, you could start with your own thoughts then ask for feedback. It is important to let the group lead while remaining on topic and encouraging group members to explore deeper in their individual follow up sessions with trained counsellors.

1998

BE AFRAID

I will lead the blind by ways they have not known, along unfamiliar paths I will guide them; I will turn the darkness into light before them and make the rough places smooth. These are the things I will do; I will not forsake them.

ISAIAH 42:16

WHO AM I?

I just want to know why
I can't find what's real
days of searching left to feel
my heart breaking
and my soul aching
eyes grown old
full of needs untold

I just want to know why
what are the reasons for my pain
no one to lose and nothing to gain
going nowhere fast
lost in circles everlast
chasing the end
searching for a friend

I just want to know why
I can't find that level
that all seen in me is the devil
that I love so sweet
yet yearn to defeat
that I hate so strong
yet return to all along

all I ask are the whys
for the distrust and the lies
for the doubt and the deceit
why must I repeat

who am I
that I can't find what's real
can't stand the hurt – don't want to feel
who am I?

January 1998

My name is Shamin and I'm an addict.

My mother always said smoking pot would lead to other drugs but I thought I had all the answers. I can still remember the "good old days" before I had my first toke. I was a center basketball player, star server in volleyball, and a straight-A student. That all ended soon enough. Nowadays, I can barely get up the energy to run a block never mind a basketball court. I went from ninety-seven percent in French to being expelled because I thought I was too good for school. My friend and I would spend our morning breaks and lunch hours smoking up. I slept through all of my classes but, because I did my homework, I still got good grades. The principal was right. I should have been using school for my education – not as a hotel.

Now, seven years later, I'm an addict recovering not only from marijuana, but from mushrooms, acid, crystal methadone, mescaline, cocaine and – my most beloved and most feared – freebase (crack). I've also been a thief, con artist, and prostitute and am now a single mother struggling not only with my old habits but with the infamous Child and Family Services (CFS) as well. They have a four-month supervisory order on me and my two-month-old son, but don't think I'm naïve enough to believe that these four months is where my self-inflicted misery with them will end. They're here and they're here to stay but I have no one to blame but myself, right? You do the crime, you do the time.

All because of that first toke offered at a party by one of my closest "pals." Wow, did that have an effect on me! It became the only thing I wanted to do. In the beginning I stole money from my mom's purse and blackmailed her boyfriends to afford it. After a while marijuana just wasn't enough to give me a "good buzz" anymore. So I moved on to bigger and better.

I flew right through the "shrooms and acid" phase, or so it seemed. They just didn't seem to hit the spot like crystal methadone did for my friends. So, I tried that. Unfortunately, I kept on trying it until I weighed less than 100 pounds. For a girl of five foot seven, that isn't a very appealing weight.

Crystal, as we called it, was something of a wonder drug. Its effects lasted for days, and even though I couldn't bring myself to eat a single thing, I could talk 100 miles a minute, make friends faster than I could blink, and feel invincible – on top of the bloody world! But, it got too expensive. In actuality it was a pretty inexpensive drug, but my body developed a tolerance to it almost immediately and the costs added up.

Around that time my mom began to notice the money missing. Of course, I denied taking it. This led to some pretty outrageous arguments when, incredibly, I believed *I* was right and *she* was being unreasonable. I began to feel resentful toward her for distrusting me and believing I would do a thing like that. I sabotaged her and her relationships to do what I self-righteously thought of as "getting even" with her. Eventually, my home became an unwelcoming place, and, because I blamed my mom for the choices I had made and the problems I had, I left. That meant I left her purse as well. Hence, I began my life as a con artist.

I went downtown and picked out wealthy old men. After I gave them some kind of "damsel in distress" story they would take me home and offer me whatever they had – alcohol, food, etc. When the moment was right, I'd steal their money, jewelry and whatever else I could find that was worth something. However, the only reason I did this is because they were only out to take advantage of my young little body. After all, they knew I was underage. At least, that's the way I justified how I treated them. I may have even been right nine times out of ten but I was in the wrong and I knew it – but the guilt and shame weren't anything some drugs couldn't make better.

My dad found me downtown one day. He'd assumed I was "hooking" and began to preach about the dangers of being a "working girl" and how they only did more drugs to hide from what they'd become. He also reminded me of my potential. He bestowed kisses, love and concern on me and offered his understanding and his help. I wasn't ready, though, to accept what he offered because then I'd also have to accept what I'd become. On the one point, he was right – I was hiding from myself. On the other, I was outraged that he thought I'd become a prostitute. I allowed my outrage to grow to a boiling fury. In doing this, I had the courage to walk away from him as I had from my mom – and was able to defend myself from the truth.

Feeling as though I had no one left who understood me, I struck out at the nearest person – me. I began using mescaline and cocaine. I stayed in dealers' homes and took almost any drug that came my way, including Ecstasy. Fortunately, I never did anything that I regretted while on it – sexually that is.

As the months grew into one another, so did my habits. I became tired. Tired of living, tired of loving. Tired of hurting and being hurt. I grew scared. Scared of being alone, being judged, and being rejected. Most of all, I grew scared of drugs.

With the help of family, I moved to a new city – away from old "friends." I stayed with my aunt and went back to school. I've now finished grade twelve.

So, that's it? you're asking. That's the end? No. It isn't. Addiction is a disease. One that cannot be cured, one that never goes away. I was clean for almost two years before I relapsed. I thought I'd kicked the habit. I thought I could have control. I was wrong.

I started using cocaine – free-base. Weed would've been too weak for me – I'd already been through too much. I was offered "just one toke" but I took many more after that. I dropped out of college to pursue my habit. At first, everyone was "nice" to me. Everything was free – so I never took it seriously until it was too late. Within months I became a prostitute like many of my "friends" were.

On the streets I met my "knight in shining armor." He wasn't a customer. He was just there. Every time we met, he'd ask for a chance to help me. I always walked away. Then one night he was waiting for me at a crack house I frequented. The others kept offering him "just one toke," and he kept on saying "no." For that I admired and respected him; I envied his strength. I went home with him that night.

We were together on and off for a little over a year. Eventually, he began to use with me because, he said, those were the only times I stayed at home with him.

Four months into our relationship we discovered I was pregnant with his child. I still "worked" – and each day I grew to hate myself more. I still used because I had to hide from my hatred. I would tell myself this and make myself believe it. We began to verbally and physically fight.

I began to feel my child move within me when I was five months pregnant. I couldn't bring myself to continue hurting us. I went through both detox and rehab. I gained thirty pounds and was clean for two and a half months.

My boyfriend was an addict-in-denial by this time. I couldn't help but feel that I was to blame for this, so I wouldn't leave him. I loved him too, I think – for being there for me and loving me. I relapsed. Within two weeks of starting drugs again, I was deeper into my addiction than I'd been the entire time I'd used. The weight I'd recently put on fell off my bones like water runs off your body in a shower.

Fortunately, I grew wary of my addiction as quickly as I had fallen back into it. I quit drugs for what I believe is the last time. Two weeks after I quit, CFS contacted me, and I've been working with them ever since. My boyfriend and I are separated and have recently given up hope of working things out. Every day has been a struggle. We've tried not to let ourselves wallow in the past because it causes so many negative emotions to surface – toward each other and ourselves. It's been very hard, though. After all, the past has made us who we are today.

Writing this has brought back memories. It's made my hands shake and my stomach tighten. It's made me want to get high, with a fierce and aching need, and it has made me proud – because I have the strength to resist that "need."

You may be questioning why I chose to share my story. I didn't do it because I want you to hate drugs. I want you to fear them. To hate something means we avoid it because we despise it; to fear something means we avoid it because we know it will hurt, or possibly kill, us.

I don't hate drugs and I don't think that I ever will – but I will **always** fear them.

Self Reflection Guide

1. Have you ever used drugs?
2. Do you have other addictions? (alcohol, food, sex, money, approval)
3. What was good about yourself and/or your life before you began to experience trouble with the addiction of your choice? How has your life changed? What have you lost?
4. I pushed my parents away when I needed them most because I was angry and ashamed. When have you pushed someone away when you needed them? Why?
5. All addictions have a progression; my lifestyle got gradually worse. From marijuana use to crack use to prostitution and so on. What has been the progression in your life?
6. Among other things, I stole from my parents, blamed and rejected them, robbed men, sold myself, isolated myself and became involved with an abusive partner. What has your lifestyle led you to do that you would not have done otherwise?
7. When have you been confronted by a truth you couldn't accept? How did you respond? If you could do it over, what would you do differently?

ACTIVITY

Using pictures, words, or whatever else you would like, create a collage of the things you lost. (See question #3.) Use the collage as a reminder of God's promise to you. These are the things God wants to bring back into your life – and He will.

AUGUST 2000

ALWAYS AND FOREVER

On hearing this, Jesus said to them, "It is not the healthy who need a doctor, but the sick. I have not come to call the righteous, but sinners.

MARK 2: 17

COCAINE HIGH

More! I want more.
Heart throbbing, head pounding
Mouth dry, and lips chapped
Consumed by my insatiable need

More! I want more.

Aaah, Sweet heat sliding down my throat
Smoky os of euphoria slipping from my mouth
Eyes closed in sweet rapture… and then…

More! I want more.

Eyes huge, pupils dilated
Emotions racing, mind raging
Conquered – by my inevitable weakness

More! I want more… of that
COCAINE HIGH

August 2000

No! I thought I'd closed this chapter of my life yet here I am sitting in a crack house begging for "just one more hit" before I go. I've changed. The whole "game" has changed. It's not fun anymore. Ever since I gave up my son for adoption, I've been on this crazy roller coaster – trying to stay clean – but for what? For who? And what am I supposed to do, if I'm not doing this?

I look like crap now. I'm so skinny, so dirty. I didn't even brush my teeth today – or yesterday. I haven't changed my outfit for almost a week and the last time I remembered to eat was two days ago. I had a breakfast drink and a pizza pop. Lord Jesus, what am I doing? What have I become? I'm nothing… nobody… and I'm alone. If only…

I don't even really remember when I started up again – or why. All I know is that I've been to every treatment center there is, and I must not really want to be clean because I can't seem to stay that way. Life sucks. I'm starting to feel real sorry for myself these days. I've got no friends, no family, no man – no one I can turn to, no one I can trust. Then again – I can barely trust myself.

I'm working the streets again because it's the fastest way to my next hit – that's about all it is, though. Everything I had from working escort is gone. I still see it here and there – in the pawnshops, my dealers' homes or on their girlfriends' bodies. I don't even care anymore. Sometimes I wonder if I ever did. I'm lost, I'm scared, and I am *sick and tired of this life!* Getting arrested almost seems like a good thing these days – three meals a day, a clean bed and plenty of rest. A home away from hell.

Speaking of arrest, I must have a couple of warrants out by now. I've been released on at least three PTAs (promise to appear) in the last year alone, but I haven't been to court once. There goes the banking career I always dreamed of. Oh well – I probably would've just ended up with some hard time for embezzlement. Forget it! I gotta get high!

SELF REFLECTION GUIDE

1. What have been some of the lowest points in your addiction? What did you think about yourself then? What did you say to (or about) yourself? What did you feel would have helped you? What did you want for yourself then?
2. What do you want for yourself now?
3. What can you do to achieve what you want for yourself? Can you totally abstain, and if not, can you choose to use less? It may even be a step as small as using every second day – but it is still a step towards your goal. These goals can be adjusted as time progresses. If using every second day is working out, go every third day – or every week. If using every second day is not working out, set a smaller goal – such as using only until a certain time each day, using less of the substance (like one gram instead of three) each day or using a less harmful substance instead (marijuana instead of cocaine).

This approach can work for any addiction, not just drugs. For example, someone addicted to approval may choose to practice saying how they feel once a day or saying no to things they do not want to do. What is the smallest step you can take towards what you want for yourself?

ACTIVITY

Feel your emotions. Cry, yell (outside or into a pillow), hit something (a pillow) sing (make up words as you go). Channel your emotions into something creative: keep a journal, write a song, poem or letter, draw or paint a picture, dance.

October 2001

Sharing the Moment

He will wipe every tear from their eyes. There will be no more death or mourning or crying or pain, for the old order of things has passed away.

REVELATION 21:4

I AM ALONE

I am alone
Alone with God
He's walking with me
He's talking with me
My mind's at rest
My soul's at ease

I am alone
Alone with God
Didn't even pray
But he's with me today
I feel him inside
I have nothing to hide

I am alone
Alone with God
He's holding me
He's molding me
My heart is content
My spirit joyful

I am alone
Alone with God
Never tell him where
But he's always there
Always holding my hand
Beside him I stand

I am alone
Alone with God

October 2001

Everyone in an addiction lifestyle reaches a point of giving up. Such people can give up on one of three things: on themselves (through surrendering to drugs), on life (through suicide), or on their lifestyle (through quitting drugs). My self-disgust and hopelessness led me to give up on each of these things at various points throughout my addiction. Yet, for reasons I'm only now beginning to understand, part of me that refused to let go of who I had been before drugs consumed me. That part of me knew that "the moment" would come when I would be given strength beyond my own, strength to overcome the obstacles I had created for myself. I would like to share that moment.

It was only two weeks after I'd gotten out of my latest treatment program – the only one I'd managed to complete – and I was already in the middle of a relapse. This one was the worst setback yet. I was so hard up to get high that I could barely take myself out of the crack house to go and make money. Instead I begged my dealers and their customers for handouts until I was told to leave. I had no shame, no pride – and respect had become a word without meaning. As bad as it was I had myself believing that I'd grown healthier habits because I could no longer go twelve to fourteen days without rest and food.

When my insatiable thirst for milk and my constant weariness caused my dealer to become concerned about a possible pregnancy, I went to the doctor and found out I was already four months along. I went home in a state of horror. How could I be pregnant? What should I do? You would think the answers should be obvious and that I would quit living as I was but, no, I put on my best outfit, made some quick cash, and got high. I wanted to remain lost in the insanity of my one-track mind and avoid facing the reality of the situation. To stay high, I had to change my clothes and "get beautiful" again. When I got home I tore off my clothes and stormed into the bathroom naked – But I never made it to the shower.

You see, my home had become a shrine to my son, Jerome (not his real name). His pictures were everywhere – in the bathroom, on the fridge, the cupboards, and every wall. I had avoided seeing them for this long by staying high until I passed out with the pipe in my hand. I had not given myself time to grieve or deal with the guilt and the shame that I associated with losing him. Crack had been my cure, my nightly remedy for the problems of life. I wasn't high enough not to see them this time. They were staring at me while I stood naked, staring back, and I kept thinking he was so small, so innocent, so trusting. He'd loved his mommy so much and I had failed him. I'd chosen drugs over my own child.

Something within me broke open then, like a little door I never knew was there. I was engulfed by sob after horrible sob as I ran into the living room in an effort to escape my pain. It was uncontrollable. All I knew at that very moment was that I hurt with a terribly indescribable ache and that the only choice I had left was to face it. I walked through each room, looked at each picture and relived each precious moment I'd had with my son. I wanted to die, and yet, never more in my life had I wanted to live. I spoke to those pictures – I told them of my sorrow, my regret, and I vowed to do better this time, to be there for my child.

I wasn't sure if I could do it. My faith in myself had been lost, and the unbearable desire to get high – which I was struggling against even at that moment – had me trapped in terror. I cried harder because of my obvious weakness, unconquerable helplessness, and the belief that I was hopeless. I didn't think I'd be able to overcome my cravings. I crumpled to the living room floor, cradling my naked body in my arms and, in total desperation, cried out to God for help. Out of fear and anger came the outspoken admission that I couldn't do it on my own.

"Please God, just help me get through the night. I can't go back out there – I don't want to lose this baby. I can't go through it again! I got up on my hands and knees and crawled determinedly into my bed. Still crying and holding myself I asked once more, "Please, God, please. Just hold me. Hold me 'til I fall asleep. Please."

Instantly, the most amazing thing happened. My tears dried up, my cravings faded, and I was consumed by a feeling of utter peace. It was as though God held me. I remember thinking, before I fell asleep, that He had heard me and He had come.

For the longest time I was unable to share that experience with anyone. I knew it would be unbelievable and sound crazy. However, it's been six months and He is still with me when I can't do it alone. I am clean, I am happy and I am loved. Most importantly, I am never *ever* alone.

I am grateful for these last six months but I know that I have to continue to stay close to God and I work hard at doing so. I know that to walk away from Him who has been the light will only lead me in one other direction – toward the dark.

SELF REFLECTION GUIDE

1. Think about the times when you gave up. What did you give up on? (self, life, addiction)
2. Choose two of the following and reflect on them:

    When you gave up what did it look like?

    When you gave up what did it sound like?

    When you gave up what did it feel like?
3. What are the things in your life that make you want to keep trying?
4. What gives you strength and comfort in difficult times?

    (prayer, exercise, art, music, writing, dancing, singing, talking to someone, art, cooking)
5. Part of me refused to let go of who I had been before drugs consumed me. That part of me knew that 'the moment' would come... The part of me that refused to let go was called *hope*. Is there a part of you that refuses to let go?

ACTIVITY
Think about why you refuse to let go? What do you hope for?

VERSES TO CONSIDER:
Who hopes for what he sees? But if we hope for what we do not see, we wait for it with patience. - Romans 8:24b, 25

Rejoice in hope, be patient in affliction, faithful in prayer. - Romans 12:12

With God all things are possible. - Matthew 19:26

NOVEMBER 2001

BREAKING THE SILENCE

Then you will know the truth, and the truth will set you free.

JOHN 8:32

THE LITTLE GIRL

she's locked away beyond the darkness of her time
molded by a past long gone and yet forever captured in her mind
SHE WAS NOT MEANT TO SUFFER!

she is not a toy
a plaything with which to practice your sexual prowess
she is not a tool
a sharpener with which to fine tune the cutting edge of your words
she is not a lesson
a sounding board for your psychological oddities
she is not inanimate
a punching bag with which to deny your inferiority or prove otherwise
AND SHE NEVER SHOULD HAVE BEEN!

she is a child
a little girl locked behind a door of starkness
of black and ugly anguish; pain beyond her knowledge or control
and I hear her cries
wails of untold anguish; sobs of untouched shame
bewildered moans of doubt; recriminating screams of blame
with each dawn, I hear her anger and her sorrow
with each sunset, I hear her hope – her faith in tomorrow

I go to her at times
meaning to leave ajar the door – let in some light
to take away the terrors of the day – to heal the horrors of the night
but I cannot
mind shriveling in a race to escape – I rush to close the door instead
to let her suffer
THE LITTLE GIRL LOCKED INSIDE MY HEAD

November 2001

I'm in group therapy for childhood sexual abuse now. I've been clean for seven months and writing this is helping me to accomplish three things: I'm completing another chapter; I can share it in group tonight; and the silence I've held for so long will have finally been broken. As I was growing up, I experienced so much sexual abuse that I'm not sure I even remember it all. Wow, where do I start? When and with whom?

I was abused by my neighbor, my music teacher and my auntie. The odd thing about this is that, in each situation, I was never one hundred percent certain that I could call it abuse.

When I was eight years old, my neighbor offered me a ride on his riding lawn mower. I didn't know him well, but he seemed harmless and he even offered to let me "drive" (steer). So I sat on his lap and steered while he fondled my vagina beneath my pants and asked me, "Do you like that?" I was confused. I didn't know if he meant the ride or the touching, so I just nodded my head. I remember the absolute bewilderment I felt on my way home and the shame and then the guilt I felt when my entire immediate family confronted him after I told about the incident. He appeared so shocked at our accusations that I began to doubt myself and pity him.

When I was nine years old, my music teacher kept me in after class and locked the doors. I had a hole in the crotch of my pants and he commenced showing me how to "sew" it by first fingering the hole and then folding down my pants and running his hands along their seam while making sure that the backs of his hands were pressed and moving against my vagina. Again, I told. We went to court and I won. He was a strong community leader and involved in many committees involving interaction with children. After court, I felt as though I had not only ruined his marriage and his reputation but that I had further violated myself (and my privacy) through the constant repetition of my story to stranger after stranger. I vowed never to go through that again.

When I was eleven years old, I was living with my auntie. I used to give her back massages almost nightly. Every once in a while she'd complain about cramps, and one day I massaged inside her vagina to help ease them. She never stopped me and I never told. The cramps began to come more often, and the massages didn't end.

As a teen, I was abused by my friend's father and by my uncle.

When I was seventeen, I stayed the night in a hotel with my girlfriend and her dad. We were celebrating her birthday. I woke up in the middle of the night with him grunting quietly on top of me and thrusting between my legs. I never told. I felt resigned to what had been happening throughout my life. I gave up on trying to believe I could lead a normal one. I began to think that my body was meant for that – whether I liked it or not.

On my eighteenth birthday, my uncle took me out for the entire day. By that time, I was heavily into drugs and he bought us a few eight balls of cocaine and rented a hotel for the evening. The first half of the evening was spent getting high together. Then I started to get out of control, wanting more and more cocaine. He held back the drugs to increase my desperation. He asked for sex in exchange for the rest of the cocaine but I said no. I tried to reason with him – he was my uncle and it wouldn't be right – but my desperation got the best of me so I made a compromise. I crawled into the bed, naked, and played with myself for him. He got naked and began masturbating as I did this. I ended up getting the drugs without having to have sex or personally service him in any other way but I began to really hate myself that day. I felt dirty, ashamed, guilty and confused all at once. I told my aunt (whom I was living with again) and she blamed me for leading him on, dressing and acting the way I did around him. I moved out the next day.

As an adult, I abused myself. I became a prostitute. I'd had all the training I could ever need and I had enough self-loathing not to care about how it hurt, each time, to lie motionless beneath some faceless grunter. I told myself that it was the only way to have control – and I had money to buy the drugs that took it all away and made life "better."

When I first got off cocaine I completely blamed myself for my adult abuse but therapy has helped me see that those men were at fault. I made no secret of my age or my addiction and, like my uncle, they took advantage of a vulnerability that I didn't know was there and a weakness I felt helpless to overcome. Today I am growing. I love myself. I know that I deserve better than what I've had in the past and I demand it from the present. I am healing and I am also hurting – but I can face the truth now. It happened, it hurt, and it was wrong – but it wasn't my fault alone.

Self Reflection Guide

1. This chapter talks about sexual abuse but abuse can take many forms. It can be emotional, mental, cultural, verbal, physical, sexual, financial, spiritual, neglect, abandonment and so much more. The basic definition of abuse is to treat or use something (or someone) improperly. Have you experienced abuse?

2. As you read the poem, what were your thoughts? Could you relate to any of it? What parts did you connect with most?

3. When the man who abused me when I was eight years old appeared shocked by my family's confrontation, I began to doubt myself and feel ashamed. Has there been a time in your life when you've tried to confront someone about inappropriate behavior and the person has made you feel as though it was your fault or, even worse, as if you imagined it or made it up?

    a. Do you think it was my fault?

    b. Was it in my imagination or made up?

4. In many ways, the court process revictimizes survivors by making them relive the trauma over and over again and making them feel as though they are the ones on trial and have to prove that they are telling the truth. Sometimes it can feel like speaking up is pointless. Have you ever experienced this in court, with service providers, family, friends or anyone else you have reached out to for help?

    a. How did this affect you (feelings, decisions, behavior)?

    b. What could others have done to support you? What did you need?

      c. Was there anything you did to take care of yourself that was not harmful? (eg. talk to someone, journal, affirmations)

      d. What could you do to take care of yourself now?

5. After a while, I began to believe that my body was meant for the sexual pleasure of others. How have your beliefs about yourself been affected?

6. I was abused by many people with different forms of authority over me. These were people that I was supposed to be able to trust (teachers, family, friends' parents). Who has broken trust in your life? How?

7. As adults we carry the pain from our abuse with us. It affects how we see ourselves and the world around us. It influences our choices and how we cope in life. How has it impacted how you cope?

      a. What are the harmful ways you cope?

      b. What are the helpful ways you cope?

ACTIVITY

Write a list of the positive ways that you cope with negative thoughts and feelings or stressful circumstances. Research ways to cope (go online, talk to others) and add ideas that you like to your list. Make three copies of this list. Keep one copy of your list with you and post the other two in your home where you can see them. Read them as often as you can. Practice them, and notice which items work better. You could also give a copy to someone you trust and ask that person to remind you of your coping options when you are feeling overwhelmed.

MARCH 2002

SLIPPIN' AND SLIDIN'

*Now faith is confidence in what we
hope for and assurance about what we
do not see.*

HEBREWS *11:1*

STRUGGLING

i am lost
lost in self-hatred, embraced in darkness
lost in a tunnel without light
struggling
when will i win? or will i?
i am scared
trapped in solitude
my core is screaming, drowning in tears
yearning
tears for then, for yesterday, for her
i am her
doubtful, confused
entrenched in misery
wondering
i deny my shame and
i am shameful
i deny my failure
and am one
hiding
afraid of change or just afraid
i am lost
lost in self-hatred, embraced in darkness
lost in a tunnel without light
struggling

March 2002

It's been a while since I last sat down to write. I've been slippin' and slidin' through the last year. Well, it's almost been a year, anyway. My beautiful son Damiyen has been home from CFS for close to three months now. I have a TV, cable, phone and all the rest. I'm back in school studying basic computers and searching for the right career to pursue. And I'm craving – like the dickens.

I've lost touch with my spirituality and discovered myself wallowing in self-pity. I was resentful of everyone and everything because of a life of "thrills" that I can't go back to without serious consequences. I could lose my child and eventually my life and knowing this only made the cravings more potent. I've slipped twice now. Twice in one year – definitely an improvement but still not good enough. Story of my life, right? Nothing's ever good enough.

The first time I fell off the wagon was before Damiyen came home. I was drunk beyond belief and getting ready to shake my stuff for a wet T contest when I ran into some old acquaintances. One thing led to another and I ended up in the washroom of the bar sucking on a pipe. I ditched my "straight" friends shortly after – all of whom were crying and pleading with me not to do what I was about to do. I spent the next fourteen hours replaying the insanity of my addiction. Thank the Lord, I had given away my bank card before I left my friends and was therefore forced to come down to earth earlier than I would have otherwise.

I crashed hard. I was terrified by what I had done and very ashamed. CFS was giving me regular drug tests and this could mean losing my son for good. *How could I have been so stupid? So selfish?* I went to a Narcotics Anonymous (NA) meeting and told them what had happened, how I was feeling and how scared I was of losing everything I'd worked so hard for. I wept so hard that I lost my contact lenses. Thankfully, CFS didn't test me on time. I vowed to reassert my sobriety and did – for a while.

The second slip was on my birthday. Another old acquaintance got out of jail and showed up on my doorstep the day before. I very stupidly spent our time together reliving "old times" and soon found myself wishing for that sense of "freedom" again. I'd managed to completely forget how totally engulfed by insanity I'd really been; how trapped I'd been by my addiction.

I bolted from the bar on the night of my birthday. Thankfully, a friend found me at the crack house, walked me home, and talked me out of my stupidity. The damage was done, yes, but at least I was able to get myself back under control within an hour or two. On returning home I asked the old acquaintance to leave, and I resumed my fight for sobriety.

This is a battle that may never truly end but I *will* win. I have beautiful caring and supportive friends in my life today who want what's best for my sons and me – and are convinced that we deserve it. I'm still fretting about the possibility of a drug test... especially since I've smoked weed as well. I'm holding Damiyen in my arms right now – tangible proof that it wasn't fucking worth it to get high – and I know what I have to do.

I have to invite the Lord into my life more completely – allow him to remove the insidious desire to be in a world I hate and enable me to appreciate the glorious gifts he's given me. I have to step out of self-pity and into thankfulness, out of resentment and into love. As God is my witness, I will survive and conquer the disease of my addiction.

Self Reflection Guide

1. Although I had used only two times in that year, I focused on the imperfection – the mistakes I made – more than the progress. Can you name times where you have overlooked your success or progress because it wasn't perfect yet?
2. List things in your life that you'd like to improve – or change (e.g., smoke less, quit using drugs).
3. List the advantages and disadvantages of making this change (e.g., be a healthier parent and have better self-esteem versus coping with the emotional pain of the past and losing friends).
4. List the progress you've already made, no matter how small you think it is.
5. What are your strengths (e.g., trying to do better, know some healthy people, determined, survivor)?
6. What can you do to keep moving forward? HINT: Build on your progress and strengths in small ways (e.g., connect with healthy/supportive people more regularly, practice new coping strategies, set limits with others)

ACTIVITY

Pick the easiest thing from your list in question 2. Make a plan of action and choose a start date. If you feel comfortable, share this with someone you trust who will encourage and support you as you follow through.

JUNE 2002

STRIPPED OF MY MOTHERHOOD

The only thing that counts is faith expressing itself through love.

GALATIANS 5:6B

THIS IS WRONG

No! Please! You're wrong!
say no more, my ears are closed
what do you know?
oh, the lies you've tried to sell
as you sit and tell
me that to strip my motherhood
is for my own good
torn from my arms
like a Band-Aid from gaping wound
left to bleed and ooze agony

No! Shut up! You're wrong!
say no more, my ears are closed
who do you think you are?
I will not be sold
on this violation – he was only two days old
my kind will **forever** stand apart from yours
you with your education, no experience and opened doors
you have not lived my life
persecution, suffering and trials
known to you only through the book of God

No! Wait! You're wrong!
say no more, my ears are closed
why can't you see?
staring at me through empty eyes
pretending to empathize, waiting for my sorrow
to prove my weakness on the morrow
but I am strong and I am proud
a woman borne of agony
and you with your lack of insight
you will **have** to see
that I am right… and this was wrong

June 2002

I've been avoiding having to write this chapter for some time now. Why? I'm not sure. Maybe I think I deserve the pain I brought upon myself by the fight to be a part of my children's lives. Maybe I'm just afraid others will think I deserve the pain or maybe I'm just avoiding reliving that pain again. Either way, I'm writing it now.

It's been almost four years since I wrote the first chapter for this book. At that time I had custody of my first child, Jerome, under a supervisory order. I started using again a few months after writing it due to a lack of coping skills when it came to dealing with his abusive and chemically dependent father. I turned myself in to CFS and eventually recognized the need to give him up to a better home. He was about a year old when I did this but I made my worker promise me, in and out of court, that I would see him at least twice a year before I would relinquish my parental rights. Following this decision I hid from dealing with my grief by burying my pain in the pipe.

I missed a visit or two due to being high out of my mind (I refused to see him in that state.) I remember sending his second birthday gift by cab because I was too ashamed to let him see me high. I was so angry with myself. I wanted to see him so bad and had been so excited the week before that I hadn't bothered to get high – until the night before I was supposed to see him. I ran into some people who offered me free drugs and I convinced myself

I would be fine by the next morning. I wasn't. I was still high and wanted more. That was a difficult day for me – knowing my son was waiting for me and not feeling free to go because I knew he deserved to be with me in my right mind... not all *fucked up*!

When I became pregnant with my second child, Damiyen, I commited myself to changing my life for him and his brother so they would have a mother they could be proud of. I contacted CFS and informed them of my pregnancy and proceeded to make the necessary changes in my life. I moved into a home for pregnant women, turned myself in to the police on my outstanding charges, got a temporary job as a receptionist, started group and individual therapy, submitted urine for regular drug testing and went to NA meetings. I also contacted a lawyer and enrolled in a program focused on helping mothers who have used drugs or alcohol during pregnancy. I was afraid that CFS would take my baby without giving me the opportunity to prove myself because of my obvious mistakes with Jerome, so I was working toward preventing them from being able to.

During this time I was also making numerous efforts to see Jerome. He had been assigned a new worker, and she knew nothing about the case prior to my relinquishing my parental rights. So she didn't know about the visits I was entitled to (by law) twice a year. I wrote letters to the worker, her supervisor, my lawyers, my son, his foster parents (who were considering adopting him and not at all happy to hear from me), and Children's Advocacy. It took close to three months to clear up the misunderstanding and another two months of harassing his worker before I was granted my first real visit (outside of the CFS office).

Jerome's foster parents were intimidated by my persistent, unrelenting presence, and they chose to play it safe by agreeing to my requests with absolutely no intention of actually following through. I spent a lot of my pregnancy sobbing in my room due to cancelled visits and unfulfilled promises. Finally my anger got the best of me and I had my lawyer take them to court with the papers that demonstrated that I had been granted visitation that wasn't being allowed by the worker or the foster parents. This got my point across and my visits became less of a problem without having to even take it to a judge.

Then came the baby. At two days old, he was taken from the hospital to a shelter. I remember how bewildered I felt. After all, I had been clean for *five* months and they had come for him anyway. My heart felt like it was breaking. I spent a week grieving as though he had died. I sobbed so hard and so long that I became plagued with headaches from sunup to sundown.

Then I rolled up my sleeves and got to work proving that they had no probable cause or, in this case, no reason to believe that my child was in need of protection from me. We took the matter to court. Proceedings were adjourned for one month, both to give me time to build my case, and Damiyen's father time to get a lawyer.

At the first pre-trial hearing, CFS was asking for temporary (or permanent) custody of Damiyen. After I had a month to prove myself before the judge, CFS had nothing to use against me. They allowed a one-year supervisory order. They were also so impressed with the improvements I had made in my life since giving up Jerome that they insisted on my having sole custody before they would permit Damiyen to make the transition home. It took about a month to get the custody papers drawn up and signed and Damiyen was home a month later.

During the time he was in the care of CFS, I was permitted to see Damiyen three days a week for an hour. His father saw him right after me for the same time period. There were times, though, when the incompetence of the agency brought me to tears. Damiyen was moved three times in as many months; my visits were cancelled a few times without being rescheduled; and, worst of all, they refused to let me continue to breastfeed for close to a month while waiting on results of more drug tests. I had to buy a breast pump to keep up my milk supply during that period. It cost me two weeks' worth of groceries. When he came home it took me another two months of working with a lactation consultant and taking prescribed pills to re-establish my milk supply.

I was able to see Jerome quite often during this time. I even met his foster parents although I don't think anything really changed in regard to my relationship with them. They still allow me to see him only under the supervision of my cousin. whom they know and are friendly with.

At present, I have requested that my lawyer submit to the courts a "motion for access" so that I can see him once every three months, *without* a supervisor, on *specific* dates. I feel that I'd experience fewer headaches with this in place: no more cancelled visits, or waiting to the last minute to find out when I'll see him, or quality time disrupted by the excitement of my cousin's three children (who are *always* present at my visits).

Meantime, Damiyen is growing quickly and beautifully and has become wonderfully attached to me. He has begun to crawl, said "Daddy," and got his first two teeth – and I've been there for it all. *Thank the Lord for second chances!*

SELF REFLECTION GUIDE

1. I hid from dealing with my grief by burying my pain in the pipe. How do you cope with strong and uncomfortable emotions?

2. At times, we can self-sabotage when something that is important to us is about to happen (e.g., seeing Jerome for his birthday)
    a. Have you ever done this?
    b. How, when and where?

3. When I made the decision to begin to change my life I called Child and Family Services, turned myself into the police, moved into a residential setting for adolescent parents, and began attending therapy as well as self-help support groups.
    a. What steps have you taken (or thought about taking) towards changing how you are living?
    b. What would you still like to see change in your life?
    c. What steps can you take? Name all or any steps possible.
    d. Where are you willing to start?

4. My new social worker did not know about my visits with my son and I had to act on my own behalf (self-advocate) to get my rights recognized.
    a. Is there a situation in your life where your rights are not being recognized?
    b. What have you done to self-advocate?
    c. What else do you think you can you do?

d. List all the key players in this situation that you can think of (e.g., CFS worker, CFS supervisor, lawyer, child, foster parents, children's advocacy, judge, court). These will be the people to whom you will send copies of letters and other documentation that you might have.

ACTIVITY

Document. Document. Document. Keep written logs of all interactions that may affect the situation as well as copies of test results, assessments results, program certificates, letters from supporters, etc. Create a list of agencies and/or programs (supportive vs. non-supportive) that you are involved with (e.g., church, CFS, doctor, parenting group, anger management group, NA, AA, CA, therapist, probation officer, income assistance). You can choose to request letters of support, progress, and attendance from those on your list. They can write letters about your situation, progress, and/or needs. Save a copy of all documentation for yourself.

JANUARY 2003

REBUILDING RELATIONSHIP

I am not saying this because I am in need, for I have learned to be content whatever the circumstances. I know what it is to be in need, and I know what it is to have plenty. I have learned the secret of being content in any and every situation, whether well fed or hungry, whether living in plenty or in want.

PHILIPPIANS 4:11,12

UNTIL TIME TELLS

it's been so long since we first met
we've had so many ups and downs
more downs than ups
you've seen the demons in my heart
the darkness in my soul
you watched me struggle to win
a battle that will never end
I hurt you then
now your heart is closed
and yet you look at me
with remembered love
clouded with doubts I cannot ease
and with agonies of fear I cannot soothe
because of stories
that time has told

I have no shame
and yet I do regret my past
who I was and hope to never be again
I cannot look back
I can only move on
to pick up the pieces left behind
and put together again
that which is truly me
I can only hope
that you will forgive
what you cannot forget
see that I am healing
and, the rest, let time tell

I have emerged from self
full of love for others
and through the darkness
have discovered light

yet still you are
held back by memories
of fire
you will not get burned
I do not wish to hurt you
but to love you
to be who I am
and not what I was
in your eyes and mine
but shadows of the past remain
to cloud your soul
with fear
and your heart
with anger
and so, with a heavy heart
and a free soul
I will move on
go forward
to live life as it was
meant to be lived
and for you
I will wait and pray
until time tells

November 2001

It took me quite a while to regain the trust of my family and friends. To this day, there are still people in my life who find pleasure in reminding me of the kind of person I had become in my addiction. I cope with this by using those reminders to my benefit – to reinforce my determination to raise my child properly and live right. To renew my relationships I did nothing really but be myself and work hard at asking for help in times of craving and weakness. I proved my desire to become a new person by putting words into action.

I asked one friend to keep my bank card in times of desperation and another to stay with me through difficult evenings. I was always honest about how I was feeling and what devious thoughts were attacking my sense of peace. In turn, I helped them any way I could. I'd help them with their laundry, cook them a meal, or offer to care for their children. This was also helpful to my recovery because it kept me busy and gave me responsibilities and a sense of purpose to hold on to when I most needed it.

In regard to my family, things were a little bit stickier. In retrospect, I believe this is simply because their opinions mattered more and, of course, because I wanted so badly to redeem myself in their eyes for all the hurt and disappointment I had caused them. Also, they had given me their support quickly and trustingly so many times before that they had no doubt began to shy away from the idea of offering themselves to the humiliation and pain my previous failures had caused them.

In the beginning things were very awkward and I often felt that I didn't belong anymore. I recognized that was my fault for failing to remain in contact with them through the good times *and the bad*. Eventually I figured out that the best way to make it up to them was the same way I had made my friends believe in me again: by striving to do my best, keeping in touch and letting them know what direction I was going in at any given time.

I also had to spend a lot of time humbling myself by admitting that the choices I had made were wrong and that certain advice given to me by various people had been right. My father hasn't spoken to me since I gave up Jerome, and there are others who haven't yet accepted that my beautiful little boy is no longer a solid member of our family. They blame me, of course, and have no problem letting me know this. At these times, my heart breaks all over again and I am forced to keep a happy face on. I cannot let them know how much their accusatory gibes hurt me. I feel it's best if I show them that I have accepted my loss so that they may quickly do the same. I do not want to increase their pain or their anger.

All in all, I am happy with my relationships with my friends and my family. I feel that I have grown a lot in the past two years and I am proud of who I am becoming. I am an ambitious student, thoughtful friend and relative and the loving mother of two children – an athletic three-and-a-half-year-old and an inquisitive nine-month-old. I know there are still many hurdles to overcome, but I look forward to the challenges they will present and the strength I will gain from them. Part of me is still afraid of the future and the mistakes that are waiting to be made but I am confident that, no matter what happens, in the end I *will* come out on top… all I need is faith.

Self Reflection Guide

1. Are there people in your life who remind you of how you have "failed"? Can you use these reminders to motivate you? How?
2. What can you do to renew your relationships?
3. A support system is very important for addiction recovery.
    a. Who can you trust to support you in your recovery?
    b. How can they support you?
    c. What can you do to give back to them?
    d. Who do you want to remain in contact with and why?
4. In life there are no real "happily ever afters." There are only ups and downs.
    a. How can you make peace with the "downs" in your life?
    b. What losses in life could you benefit from working at accepting?
    c. What "ups" in life have you experienced?

ACTIVITY

Create a list of "ups" in life and celebrate one "up" every day. When you get to the end of your list, add any new "ups" you can think of, and start celebrating the list from the beginning again. Celebrate by thinking about how that "up" has added to your life, lighting a candle, praying in thanks, sharing it with a friend, having a bath, eating a special meal or whatever else you can think of to do.

SEPTEMBER 2003

BECOMING

Be on your guard; stand firm in the faith; be courageous; be strong. Do everything in love.

1 CORINTHIANS 16:13-14

FREEDOM CALLS

I feel trapped – lost in a box – unfree to be me
my vision oppressed by society
forced to conform to the majority's norm
waiting for the light to disperse the storm
every day a struggle – a fight for sight
within my core between wrong and right
looking for a way to enjoy today
without having to hold yesterday at bay
so much suffering – love unrequited
made hopeful by the promise of being united
I'm fighting to answer freedom's calls
but my voice is silence behind my walls
erected to save me from the pain of living
I must now tear them down and start forgiving
open up my hurts – lay out my heart
get out of the box – stop living apart
from who I am and who I want to be
Answer the call of God and finally be free!!

September 2003

The Lord has been calling me for quite some time now. Looking back, I'm amazed at how blind we can be to the miracles he performs in our lives. I'm not going to lie to you by saying that it was all easy going from the moment I accepted Jesus into my life because you're not stupid and that's not reality. It's a hard-knock life, but it's not about how many times you fall down. That doesn't matter. It's how fast and how often you pick yourself up that makes the real difference. I once heard something at a Cocaine Anonymous (CA) meeting that has really stuck with me: "A winner is nothing but a loser – that never quit trying." I am a winner. I always will be. I refuse to give up on myself – or my future.

I've made a lot of mistakes and I still have a lot of work to do. Damiyen has been back in the care of CFS for almost a year now; I'm working on getting funding to have a parent-child assessment done for court purposes; and I'm on the hunt for another job. But I have confidence in the Lord. He's brought me through worse things than this.

Throughout my entire journey of healing I've learned two things so thoroughly that they'll forever be a part of me. One, I can do *anything* through Jesus, who gives me strength, and two, I have to always put my trust in God and not depend on what I *think* I know but make my choices wisely, with Him in mind, and everything will work out as it should. I am a new person today.

Gone is the confused little girl betrayed by everyone she'd ever tried to love. Gone is the cold and bitter youth who learned to trust *no one* and hurt *anyone* who got too close. And gone is the fearful woman who couldn't be herself because she believed she wouldn't be accepted.

I'm a new person today. I'm full of love, laughter, and joy. I expect little from others and much from myself. I live my life to "become." I know that recovery is a process; that the end will always be just an arm's length away because with each day I conquer there's another day ahead, with each goal I accomplish there's another to take its place. I feel as though there's a light deep down inside me that glows to illuminate my path in life. All I have to do to get where I'm going is put one foot in front of the other; keep following that light. I make it a rule in my life today to walk in love. I refuse to allow myself to be poisoned by the bitterness of daily hurts and disappointments. There's something to be learned from everything – even when I don't get my way.

So today I look for the silver lining in life. I forgive what needs to be forgiven – even if I don't forget – and remember that I'm not the only one in the world who makes mistakes. We're *all* human and to be human means not having all the answers, not being right all of the time and not always making the right choices. We're not perfect. *I* sure ain't and I *know* you aren't. I accept that. I live with it and try to always look at how *I* can be a better person for the world instead of trying to change people and situations to suit myself. I'm not God. I don't have that power, but I *do* have the power to change me.

I spend my days smiling at those who aren't smiling, talking to people who seem lonely, hugging those who look like they need it, complimenting people, and just being happy to be me. I believe that kind words soothe the soul. In fact, I *know* they do because they soothed mine. I believe that people both need and deserve praise and comfort from one another. It's my desire to be the one to give it to them. And I do – whenever and wherever I can – to anyone and everyone that crosses my path.

I feel the world would be a better place if we could all just feel okay being true to who we are and stand in judgment of no one's actions but our own. Society has us living a lie. We measure others (and ourselves) by what they have and how they look rather than by who they are and what they're doing to "become." For me, success is no longer about what you do for a living, how much you earn, or what kind of clothes you wear. Success is achieved by "becoming." By completion of self. Don't get me wrong; there are times when I allow myself to be blinded by a desire to hide behind wealth and beauty. Of course I do – I'm human! But I've also noticed that when I do, or when I start judging myself (or others) by the societal yardstick, I lose my joy. I grow fearful, impatient, selfish and self-centered. But that's not who I want to be so instead I choose to focus on loving and being loved. I find myself having to make that choice repeatedly in a day, but that's okay because that's one choice that I've never regretted making. In all my life, of all the choices I've made, walking in love has, by far, been the easiest and most rewarding choice I've ever made.

I am blessed today; so thankful for everything God has done with my life. I'm in a loving relationship with a caring and supportive man; my ties with my family have solidified; I see my older child every three months now instead of every six and, although I see my younger son only once a week, the bond between he and I is unbreakable. In fact, it's grown stronger with time.

Anyway, like I said, there's still a lot of work ahead of me but that's just because life is about "becoming" – with each goal that I accomplish there will be another one to take its place. I can accept that because as it says in Philippians 4:13, I know that I can do *anything* through Him who gives me strength.

It's been years since the first chapter to this book was written and I feel the need to publically declare the denial I was in regarding my relationship with Jerome's father. He was a wonderful, well-loved, and caring man. He was also abusive. I was always making excuses for him because of my "love" for him, but now? Now I recognize the truth.

I used to think he was just loving me by trying to control my every move, that I deserved what I got because I wouldn't stop doing drugs and living so wildly. I was wrong. No one deserves to have her rights violated, her freedom of choice taken away, or her self-worth debased no matter what the circumstances are. He hurt me. Not only was I physically bruised, I was spiritually scarred. For a long time I felt I was unworthy of real love. I thought of myself as dirty, used, and damaged – unimportant and unnecessary to the world. I believed I was a bad person, that I wasn't good enough for society and could never be successful or belong to the ranks of "normal" civilization around me. I bore these scars long after he was gone. I carried them with me into the next three relationships and allowed myself to be subjected to various forms of abuse. Each man was seemingly "better" than the last in how he treated me, but not knowing my own worth made it impossible for me to demand that they treat me according to it.

I was abused. Sexually, physically, mentally, emotionally – and spiritually. I think the worst thing that could happen to a person is to not know your worth spiritually, to allow someone to tear your birthright from your soul When we are born into this world, we are born conquerors, warriors, princes and princesses. *We are born to be somebody.* To not know this or to have it taken from you – to live without hope, without faith, without direction – is to live without living. I know who I am today and what I'm worth. I am a new creation. I am a masterpiece. *And by the grace of God, I am what I am.*

Nobody can take that from me. The Lord has planted those truths so deep on the inside of me that not even Satan himself has a hope in hell of taking them away. He tries though. You bet you, he does. And I just keep reminding myself – every time that small and helpless feeling starts to creep in – that the only way he can win is if I *let* him. I am a child of God and I can do *anything* through Him who strengthens me.

Forgiveness has been a huge part of my growth as well. As long as I stayed angry and bitter with the people in my life who had hurt me, I continued to allow them to affect me. By keeping them in my thoughts and allowing the pain and distrust of my past to tarnish any new relationships I got involved in, I let their abuse live on in my life, The Lord taught me how to leave the past behind and trust in the future.

Shortly after I'd learned to do this, I was blessed with the opportunity to see Jerome's father again. I told him I loved him very much, that he had hurt me tremendously, and that I forgave him and would pray for healing from the hurts of his life that had caused the unrestrained anger in his heart. He was shocked and humbled by my words and grateful for my forgiveness. I have spoken to him since and was pleased to discover that he had begun to seek the Lord and make awesome changes to his lifestyle. Seeing the affect the Lord has had on *my* attitude and lifestyle has been an incentive to him in his own search for wholeness.

Learning to trust God has been the hardest and most important component of my growth. You see, I've come to understand that His plan for humanity is infinitely greater than anything we could ever imagine possible, so for me to continue to resist what I don't understand in favor of what I do is to deny myself His amazing grace and promises of prosperity in my life. Up until now, the Lord has been blessing me in *spite* of myself so I can just imagine how amazing my life will become now that I've acknowledged the wisdom of succumbing to His will for me. I am grateful for everything that I've seen, done and survived in my life because each experience has helped me to "become."

My experiences have taught me who I am and who I am not. Inside the hopeless, helpless, bad, damaged, unworthy and unnecessary child that I believed myself to be I have found a strong, intelligent, confident, proud, loving, and persevering young woman. Without having lived through the things that I have, I wouldn't be "me" today. And today, *I love myself.* Praise God!

Self Reflection Guide

1. Do you feel like you belong anywhere?
   a. If yes, where do you feel you belong? What gives you that sense of belonging?
   b. If there are places you don't feel you belong, why don't you feel you belong there? (Focus on attitudes of others, messages you receive about yourself, personal beliefs about yourself.)
2. Do you believe that you are valuable and have worth?
   a. Why or why not?
   b. What defines your worth (e.g. appearance, sexual ability, money, marital status, reputation, education, career)?
3. Have you ever given up on loving yourself or loving others because you felt unworthy? Describe the situation(s) that led up to this for you.
4. Have you ever allowed yourself to be taken advantage of by others?
   a. How? What did you give up (or allow into your life) that you didn't want to?
   b. Why? What did you get in exchange?
5. As a child, what negative beliefs did you have about yourself (e.g., don't belong, not good enough, too much trouble, a burden, failure, unlovable, unloved, a mistake)?
6. If you were able to meet yourself as a child, what would you want yourself to know?
   a. Why would this be important for the child to know?

      b.   How would you treat this child?

7. What was good about yourself when you were a child? What is good about you now?

ACTIVITY

Write a letter to your child-self. Encourage her and reassure her of her worth. Tell her how you feel about her.

1. What have you learned throughout your life journey?
2. What would make the world a better place for you?
3. How would this make the world better for you (e.g., safer, happier, less pain)?
4. I make it a rule to walk in love in my life (although I am not always perfect at it).
   a. If you could put it in a sentence, what would you say the rule for your life is today?
   b. What do you want the rule for your life to be?
   c. What can you do to move in this direction?

ACTIVITY

Make a list of who you are, who you want to be and who you are not. Remember that there is an ebb and flow to all of life (ups and downs). When we learn to walk, we will often fall down before we learn to run… this is part of growing so continue to be gentle and patient with yourself through it all. Keep track of how you are changing (growing) over the year.

FEBRUARY 2004

REBIRTH

For God so loved the world that he gave his one and only Son, that whoever believes in him shall not perish but have eternal life

JOHN 3:16

REBIRTH

they say I'm sad, they say I'm in pain
I have nothing to lose and everything to gain
cocaine brought me down, brought me right to my knees
now I'm begging you, Lord – help me, please
show me what I need to do
show me how to live – how to live for you
my heart is beaten, my soul is battered
my pride's been humbled, my ego shattered
You tore me down, now build me back
Your Word promises that I shall not lack
Lord Jesus, I am weak. Please make me strong
guide me in what's right – keep me from wrong
my eyes are windows to my soul
fill them with joy – make me whole
so that I may lead by the Spirit's light
others to you that are lost in the night
others, like me, whose spirit's are crying
show us the way, Lord – we're so tired of dying
thank you, Jesus, for your salvation and grace
for making me yours, for showing me my place
in the kingdom of heaven and the glory of earth
Father God, I'm so grateful, for this – my rebirth

February 2004

My earliest memories of learning anything about God are incidents of my grandmother forcing my hand into a hot oven screaming, "That's how hot Hell is!" and later on, tearing the cross off of my neck and telling me that there was no point to my being a Christian if I was going to be bad at it. In my later years, I became a cocaine addict, a prostitute and the victim of more than one domestically abusive relationship. My only connection to anything even close to spiritual was my relationship with my Christian cousin.

Throughout all the years that I struggled with life and through all the choices I'd made (and sins committed) she was always there – with open arms. She was my anchor, my rock – and in her, was Christ. When I talked to her about my pain and worries she would take my hand and pray. When I went to her feeling bereft and dirty, she would quote scripture and tell me that I was above it all. She never looked at me in judgment or made me feel small.

I had my own opinions about God: who He was and what He wanted from me. My cousin and I would discuss these opinions (and my fears) and she would rebuke me gently when I allowed my worldliness to diminish the reality of His omnipotence, to color Christ with the wrong tones.

My mother became born again and she was "on fire for the Lord." At first, her zeal intimidated me but later I found myself intrigued and we began to grow together spiritually.

For a long time, I felt condemned by my lifestyle and lived in constant fear of hell and damnation. Even when my addiction was the only part of my past that I still had to let go of, I felt that I could never be forgiven. I felt lost. Through my cousin, my mother, and many Christ-loving others, the Lord showed me how to forgive myself and allow my healing to become a reality to me.

I am still fighting CFS for custody of my children. *I am believing for a miracle.* I want my sons to be raised to know and love the Lord. Not the God of wrath and condemnation that I knew as a child but He who loved the world so much that he gave His only begotten son so that whoever believes in His should not perish but have everlasting life.

Today, I truly believe that I have been blessed with eternal life – that my sins are forgiven – and I want everyone and anyone who is willing to listen to know that *they are entitled to the same blessings.* I want them to feel it deep inside themselves. The only way that I know of to do God's work is to walk in His footsteps, to walk in love.

Self Reflection Guide

1. What do you believe in? (God, Buddha, love)
2. What were your early experiences with religion, spirituality and/or faith? How did this affect your faith?
3. Are there any people who strengthened your faith, were role models/mentors to you in your faith or simply believed in you as a person?
    a. How did they treat you?
    b. What was their attitude toward you?
    c. If there was no one you have experienced this with, what would you like it to look like if it happened in the future?
4. Are there (or have there been) people who saw something in you that you couldn't see in yourself? What did they see (strength, kindness, generosity, intelligence, beauty)?

I believe that it is every person's right to choose his or her own faith and that, more importantly, the act of believing in something opens us up to God and allows Him to begin to work in our lives and call us to Himself. I believe that, without faith in a Higher Being, we are lost and live without direction or meaning.

    I did not receive the Lord until I was 19 years old. Before that, I simply believed that God was love and that love was the force behind all creation, life, healing and joy. Shortly after I became a Christian, my belief was confirmed through His word when I found 1 John 4:8, "Whoever does not love does not know God, *because God is love*"(emphasis added.) This has led me to value God's gift of free will; I trust Him to work in His way, in His time. It is Love that has saved me and changed my life. It is God.

ACTIVITY

Write a list of positive things that others see in you that you do not see in yourself. Write a list of positive things that you want others to see in you that they don't (e.g., lovable, strong, kind, responsible). Using the list, write affirmations and read them out loud regularly (e.g., "I am lovable, I am strong, I am responsible.")

About the Author

Shamin, mother of three, is a poet, author and songwriter who shares her life experiences in the hope that her story will help to break down the walls of marginalization and social isolation that have kept the voices of so many women and children with stories like hers silenced behind shame.

Shamin recognizes that her journey is not over and she embraces the healing process, recognizing that there is purpose in her pain even as she continues to discover her voice and learn to walk in her truth. She has completed a university degree in social work and volunteers her time speaking with sexually exploited and at-risk youth, their service providers and other members of the public. Adopting a holistic and personal approach, Shamin uses her experiences to build bridges, create self-awareness and emphasize the inherent value and strength of marginalized women and youth.